AF413384

Today is the day

Acknowledgment

First and foremost, I would like to express my deepest gratitude to my beloved wife. Your unwavering support, patience, and love have been my rock throughout all of my adventures. Without your encouragement and understanding, this book would not have been possible. Thank you for always believing in me.

To my three sons, you are my inspiration and my joy. Your curiosity, energy, and boundless enthusiasm remind me daily of the importance of storytelling and imagination.

This book is dedicated to you, my family, with all my love - A.G.

Printed in the United States of America
First Printing, 2025

Andrew Gozzo PUBLISHING

Today is the day

By

Andrew Gozzo

Illustrated by

Kevin Richter

It's time for bed and off to sleep,
A kiss and a hug, soon to dream deep.

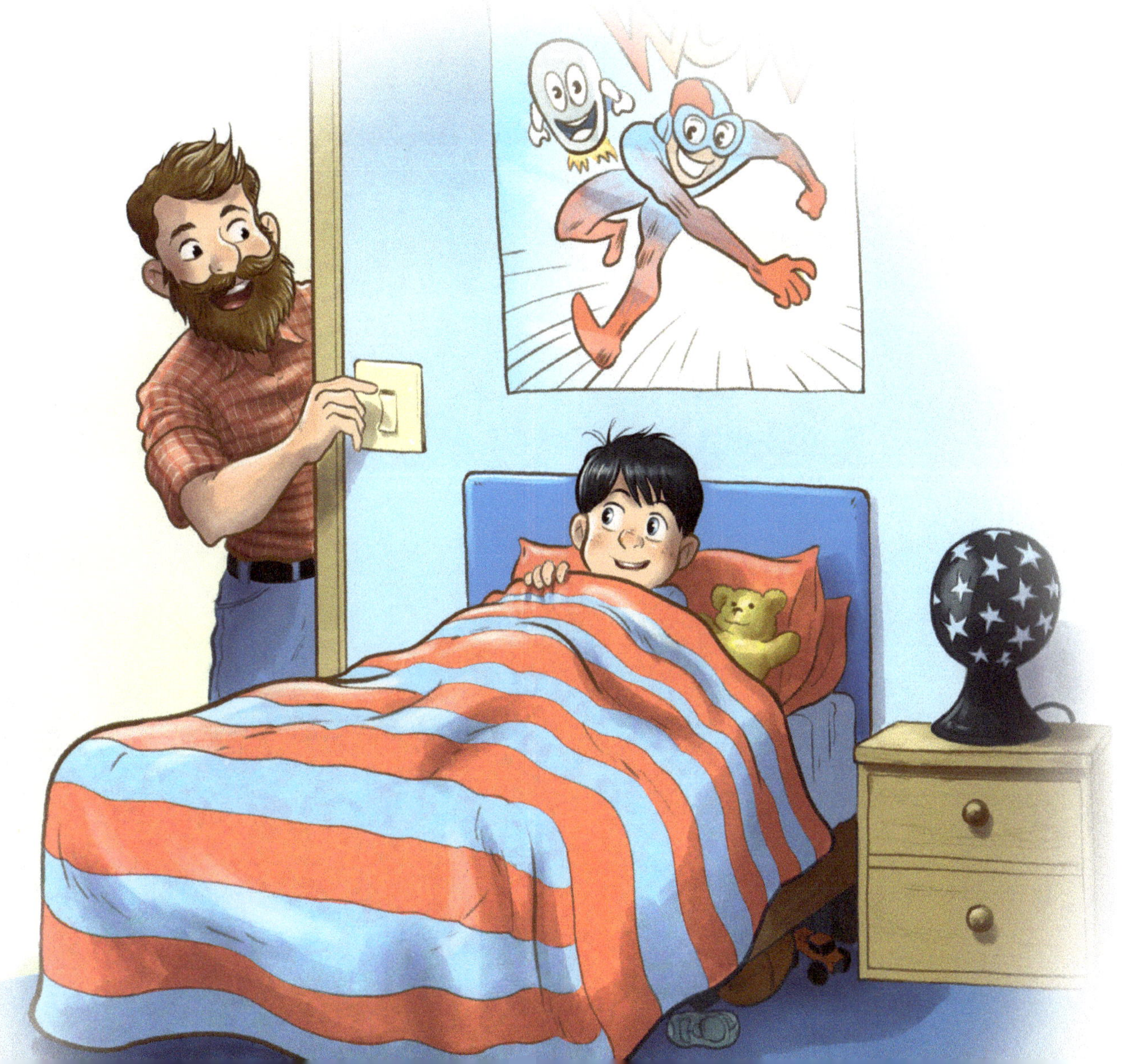

Before the lights are turned off tonight,
My dad shared with me, a bit of delight.

That he, my brother, and I next Saturday
Will have an adventure, a true getaway—

A day of fishing, just the three of us,
A big boys' getaway, without any fuss.

Now it's time to sleep, quiet and still,
I'm not sure I can—oh, what a thrill!

Tomorrow is Monday, the first day of the week;
How can I change that? It's Friday I seek.

I wake up, go to school, eat dinner, take a shower,
Soon it will be bedtime, I think, within the hour.

Tomorrow is Tuesday; are we halfway done?
"Not quite," says my dad, "but it won't be long, son."

Today was over, in the blink of an eye,
Like a jet in the sky, the day sped by.

Tomorrow is Wednesday; it can't be long now.
I'll make it to morning, but I don't know how.

How can I think of breakfast and a classroom?
I raced through dinner and showered in a zoom.

Brushed my teeth and hit the rack—
Thursday is next, and I'm not looking back.

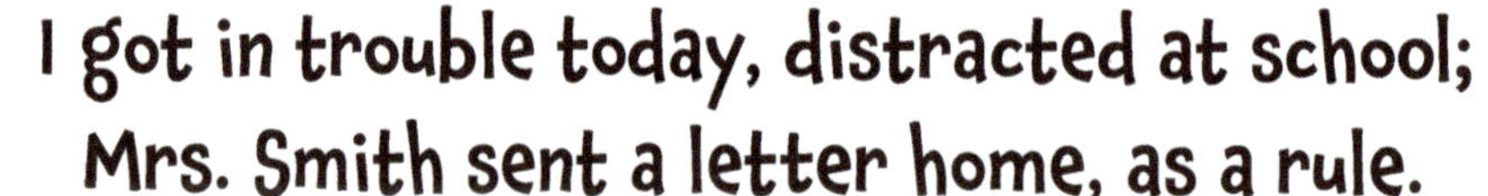

I got in trouble today, distracted at school;
Mrs. Smith sent a letter home, as a rule.

Dad read it, and he wasn't very happy, you see—
Fishing will be canceled, and it's all up to me.

Finally, it's Friday, just one day to go—
I got three gold stars for me to show.

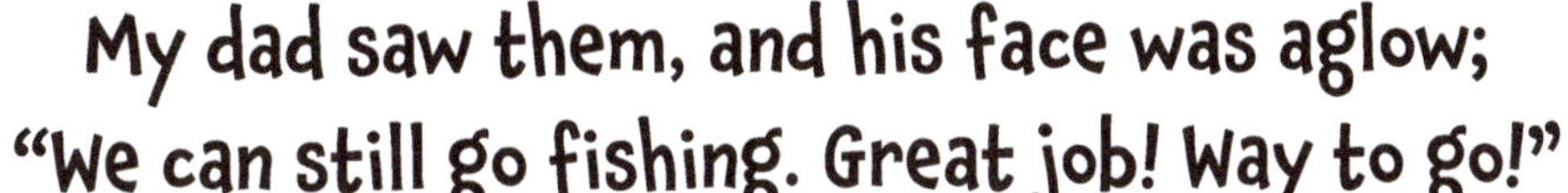

My dad saw them, and his face was aglow;
"We can still go fishing. Great job! Way to go!"

My eyes are open, I'm lying in bed—
Today's the day, just like Dad has said.

I jump out of bed and run to my brother;
He is asleep, and snoring, deep under the cover.

I crawl up next to him, sly as a fox—
"Can you please help me with both of my socks?

I need to get dressed, the rest of the way,
And eat breakfast, to start my day."

Now to my dad, who is sound asleep,
But first, I have to get past his counting sheep.

I'm on the bed, between Mommy and Dad;
He opens his eyes, but only just a tad.

"Good morning, Dad! Today is the day
That my brother, my dad, and I can play."

"yes, it is," he says to me with a smile.
"It's 4 AM; it will be just a while."

Before I knew it, my brother was ready to go;
My dad was outside, hooking up the tow.

We drove for what seemed like an hour or two,
So long that somehow I lost my shoe.

Finally, we get there, with poles in hand,
On a boat, in a lake, away from the land.

Laughing and talking, we caught not a thing—
The music was playing, we all start to sing.

"The best day ever," I say, "Can't you see?
All with my brother, my dad, and me."

About the Author

Andrew Gozzo is a dedicated father and husband with a rich tapestry of life experiences, that show in his writings.

As a proud member of the United States military, he developed a deep sense of discipline, and honor. His military service has not only honed his leadership skills, but provided the backbone of his storytelling.

A life long learner, Andrew believes in the need to pass on stories that challenge the imagination and elicit emotion and a sense of togetherness.

Family is at the heart of Andrew's life. He is married to his beloved wife and has 3 incredible sons. As a family, they enjoy activities that include game playing, camping, reading, music, joking and laughing.

Andrew is deeply grateful for the family, friends and readers that fuel this journey and make it worthwhile.

Andrew Currently lives in San Jose California, where he continues to write, learn, and explore new ideas.

About the Illustrator

Kevin Richter has worked in various creative jobs throughout his career but has found his true passion in illustration and cartooning. He lives with his wife and their two sons in the beautiful English town of Royal Tunbridge Wells in Kent.

Visit Kev at www.kevtoon.com

www.ingramcontent.com/pod-product-compliance
Lightning Source LLC
Chambersburg PA
CBHW040736150726
48196CB00011B/618